THE MYSTERY OF DIVINE FAVOR

LADEJOLA ABIODUN

THE MYSTERY OF DIVINE FAVOR

———

Ladejola Abiodun

CONTENTS

This book is dedicated to God Almighty, the giver of all knowledge and our Saviour, the Lord Jesus Christ.

INTRODUCTION

Scripture declares that *"Thou shalt arise and have mercy upon Zion: for the time to favour her; yea, the set time is come"* (Ps. 102:13) This is your time to be favoured.

We are living in the days of God's manifold grace and favour. Experience shows that a lot of people, due to sin, ignorance or demonic influences fall short of the privileges of enjoying His divine riches and favour. This ought not to be so.

This book was written to challenge you to lay hold unto the Rock that never fails — Jesus Christ. In addition to the word therein, it is also filled with prayers to strike down the strange forces of darkness against your life and vision, so that you can joyfully dwell under and enjoy the full benefits of the aura and beauty of divine favour.

God bless you.

Ladejola Abiodun

THE MYSTERY OF DIVINE FAVOR

Divine favour is God lifting a man from nothing to something.

The scriptures declare *"Thou shalt arise and have mercy upon Zion: for the time to favour her, yea, the set time, is come."* (Ps. 102:13)

I don't know how many opportunities you have lost in the past or how many people and men of God that have prayed for you but I know that now is your appointed time.

The passage above talks about the mercy of God upon Zion. The Zion in this passage of the bible is you, the church and the children of God who have been redeemed. A life without favour is a life without flavour. It is a life full of suffering, a life of trials and errors, but when favour comes, it will overrule your mistakes. Mercy, grace and favour is God's gift to man meant to see him through life.

They work together. When one comes upon you, you become a different person.

Joseph was reduced to a slave but overnight, favour lifted him - His lot was changed. Whatever you have been suffering from, grace, mercy and favour of the Lord shall come upon you and be with you from today onwards, for as soon as Joseph's master saw that the Lord was with him, he made him his overseer. Joseph was actually well favoured for the Lord was with him and he prospered in everything he laid his hands to do.

When favour comes upon you, there is no way prosperity would not locate you, no matter what you do for a living.

In Daniel 1:9, we read, *"Now God had brought Daniel into favour and tender love with the prince of the eunuchs"*. Daniel requested for an unusual food and still he was granted his request at the risk of the steward's job. From today, no human being shall turn down your good and purposeful request again.

When favour is at work, victory and deliverance is assured, no matter the number of people against you. Favour is the flavour that adds colour to a man's labour. Favour is far greater than pound sterling (the highest currency in the world). Favour will make you to overtake and recover whatever you pursue. It increases your speed of success and makes the impossibilities possible.

Psalm 30:7 *"Lord by thy favour thou hast made my*

mountain to stand strong: thou didst hide thy face, and I was troubled."

This means that nothing is impossible with a favoured man. Barriers and obstacles disappear when they see a man who is favoured. You shall be favoured from today! Favour makes people conclude that you are superior.

Favour makes your enemies submit to you. A brother was asked by his friends the secrets of his blessings because he was very rich and a Christian. He told them to prepare and come on Sunday morning so that he would take them to the source of his success. They came as scheduled and off the man drove them into the church auditorium.

In Luke 2:52, Jesus the Son of God needed favour and He got it. *"And Jesus increased in wisdom and stature and in favour with God and man"* When favour comes, increase follows. He increased in wisdom and favour before God and men. You shall find favour before God and man, in Jesus Name.

The mother of Jesus was also highly favoured from God. This means that favour has grades. Because you are going through this message, you shall be highly favoured wherever you go!

Psalm 5:12 *"For thou LORD, wilt bless the righteous; With favour wilt thou compass him as with a shield"* This passage gives me the assurance to tell you that from this season onwards, you shall be encompassed and clothed with favour, in Jesus' Name. Amen!

Proverbs 14:35 *"The king's favour is toward a wise servant: but his wrath is against him that causeth shame"*

Any one reading this message must receive favour from kings. Many captives have become captors because of favour. Many slaves have become masters because of favour. Ruth received favour which made her a fore-mother of Our Lord and Saviour, Jesus Christ.

Favour is to see and receive the good things in the land of the living. Favour also means to be treated special, a situation where you are called out of a crowd and treated with special interest without your meriting it.

30 THINGS TO KNOW ABOUT FAVOR

The following are 30 crucial insights you need to have about favor:

1. Favour is a divine product from heaven that brings sweatless victory.

2. Favour is a divine endowment that makes the face of a man to shine.

3. Favour can go ahead of you to make crooked places smooth.

4. Favour is a divine ladder to the top.

5. Favour eliminates struggling and replaces it with smoothness.

6. Favour helps a man to find a good wife Prov. 18:22.

7. Favour opens closed doors.

8. Favour is divine preference to be preferred.

9. Favour is heaven pampering you.

10. Favour is to be singled out from the crowd for help or assistance.

11. Favour is decorating your life with good things.

12. Favour makes those who don't like you to like you.

13. Favour makes people to go out of their way to give you whatever you need.

14. Favour is heaven supporting you.

15. Heaven makes your helpers unable to sleep until they help you.

16. Favour draws attention to you.

17. Favour is the extra God added to your Ordinary.

18. Favour makes you know the deep things of the Lord.

19. Favour is to be blessed.

20. Favour is to enjoy the presence of God.

21. Favour is a divine procurement that makes you acceptable where others are rejected.

22. When you are favoured, mistakes become miracles.

23. Favor our makes you a mystery nobody can unravel

24. Lack of favour makes your small mistakes to be amplified.

25. Divine favour attracts gifts even from your enemies. The Egyptians gave gifts to the Israelites.

26. Favour helps you escape the arrows the enemy throws at you.

27 Favour makes the wall of your defence impenetrable.

28. Favour is God doing the unusual for you.

29. Favour is flowing in an unmerited blessings.

30. Favour is God speaking for you.

THE BENEFITS OF FAVOR

The following are the benefits all persons experiencing divine favor will have in their lives:

1. Restoration:

Ex. 3:21 "And I will give this people favour in the sight of the Egyptians: and it shall come to pass, that, when ye go, ye shall not go empty"

When it was time for the children of Israel to go to their promised land, God gave them great favour in the sight of the Egyptians which enabled all their requests to be granted. Whenever favour comes, it comes with increase. The Lord blessed the early church with favour and they multiplied and increased day by day (Acts 2:44-47)

2. Promotion:

In this season, your promotion is coming. If your boss

wants to make a mistake, let him start fighting you who is favoured, because he would crash.

Haman made the greatest mistake of his life by plotting evil against a favoured Mordecai. Ha'-man the master died and Mordecai took his position in the country. If your land-lord is disturbing you, let him be careful or you will buy his house because God will highly favour you. You can't plot evil against a person who is favoured and succeed.

A boss who was molesting a sister was disgraced as he tried to pass the gateman with a stolen factory meat worth N200.00. He has been passing that gateman without being searched but luck fell out on him as he had decided to be molesting a favoured sister. Unfortunately for him, it also cost him his job. Any boss who is sitting on your promotion shall be removed and disgraced and your promotion will be given to you, in Jesus name. Say this with a heart ready to receive: "Favour of God, overshadow my life."

3. Divine Protection:

Psalm 91 assures us that if we dwell in the secret place of the most high God, that no sickness can kill us. After today, any sickness in your life shall not- survive. Whatever the enemy is planning against you is in vain, for you are under the shadow of the most high God. Anybody making incan-tations and fighting for you to die shall catch fire and die!!

HOW TO OBTAIN AND ENJOY DIVINE FAVOR

If you want to obtain the favor of God, here's what you need to do:

1. Be Conscious of Favour:

Think about it, acknowledge it and always remind yourself that you are a favoured child. If you want to be rich and blessed, admire rich people. You have to know that there is an entity called favour. Favour and goodness are meant to follow you as a child of God all the days of your life.

2. Ask God to load you with Favour:

Begin from now to pray for favour. Whatever you want that you think you can't get, example, favour from your boss, commissioners and those on top, just ask God to endow you with favour that will rob and spray glory on you. When king Ahasuerus wanted a queen; different kinds of girls who were beautifully decorated were made to pass by the king.

But aspiring Queen Esther refused physical decoration and decided to be spiritually clothed with favour and physically clothed with grace. This peculiar dress code gave her the Queenly position she wanted. If you are a girl, don't try to attract your husband with your paintings and nude dress codes, for he will leave you when he finds another girl who can paint more than you. But allow your natural beauty and God's grace to attract your heart's desire.

3. **Develop Good Character:** Beauty without character is useless. Your education is rubbish without good character. Your beauty may attract a husband but your character keeps him to you forever. Your certificate may get you to the top but your character will keep you there. Don't keep bad habits but reject them. Some people can't be talked to whenever they are angry or they would eat you up. That is a bad character!

Proverbs 12:2 "A good man obtaineth favour of the LORD: but a man of wicked devices will He condemn."

A good man is one with good characters. He does not live in lies, hatred, gossips, backbiting and similar evils.

From today, try to develop good character. Some girls and even Christian girls are being gossiped about because of their bad characters. Sisters, I encourage you to develop good characters.

4. **Be Thankful Always:** In every situation you find yourself, thank God. Be full of gratitude, for many have died because of murmuring and complaints. Some people don't like singing and dancing praises to God in the church. They scorn those who fully express thankful hearts to God by dancing and singing. Don't sit among them in the church.

Have the attitude of thanksgiving. Psalm 100:4 "Enter into his gates with thanksgiving, and into his courts with praise: be thankful unto him, and bless his name" God expects you to come before him with thanksgiving. Praising God should be almost like a competition where everyone wants to praise more than the other. Some people take more time thinking about their problems and conditions instead of praising God.

A sister had an irresponsible husband. One day, the husband took the woman's jeep which she bought newly for 900,000.00 and sold it for 350,000.00. He used the money for drug abuse and smoking of hard drugs.

What a waste! Is he not a husband? Sisters don't be in a hurry, take your time and praise God instead of being in a hurry.

5. **A proof of your Appearance:** Dress the way you want to be addressed. Though you might not be all that wealthy but the little you have, maintain it. Some brothers are disqualified from job interviews because of the way they dress. Imagine a brother going to an interview with a

red coat, yellow shirt, blue tie and a black trousers. Hasn't he disqualified himself? Whatever the Lord has given you, maintain it. Some don't even brush their teeth. Cleanliness is next to godliness.

6. **Sow seed of Favour:** Cain and Abel made sacrifices but God refused Cain's own and accepted that of Abel because of his heart. Honour God with your getting, remove your tithe from your gain and not the left over. Bring all the tithes to God's store house. You can't out-give God, for the more you give, the more you are blessed. You are an extension of His hand. That which you give, you shall reap very soon.

7. **Make the kingdom of God number One:** Promote, invest, participate in the kingdom of God and He will bless you. Give to men of God, poor people and God will bless you.

8. **Try to be the Best:** Whatever your hands find to do, do it with all your heart. This is another area where most children of God find difficult. Even in the house of the Lord, they keep on complaining when works are being given to them.

9. **Learn to Relate well With People:**Relate well with your mates, peers, colleagues, younger ones and most especially, your elders. Be friendly with people. It was a slave girl that brought the healing of Naaman's leprosy via relationship. Everyone is important to you. You need

people to succeed. Don't look down on anyone no matter what.

10. **Go out of your way to bless people:**

Do something to make someone happy and favour will come your way, even when you least expected it to come.

Say this: Favour of God! Overshadow my life, in the name of Jesus.

You will become an instrument which God will be using to bring glory to his name.

PRAYERS THAT PROVOKE THE RELEASE OF FAVOR

As we enter into the session of prayer, remember the following:

(1) Become God's friend like Abraham, Isaac, etc.

(2) Worry must die in your life.

(3) You must be filled with expectation

Say this Prayer: "I am an expectant fellow"

Remember you are a sinner, give your life to Jesus Christ of Nazareth today and favour will follow you. "For to them that receive him he gave power to be called sons of God" Jn. 1:12.

Prayers to Provoke Divine Favor Upon Your Life

1. Activities of favour swallowers in my life, be destroyed, in Jesus name.

2. Evil hands chasing good things away from me, wither.

3. I pursue, I overtake and recover all my lost blessings, in Jesus name.

4. Sword of the Lord, arise and fight for me.

5. Blood of Jesus, go ahead of me and make crooked places smooth, in Jesus name.

6. Evil power sponsoring tough times in my life, die! In Jesus name.

7. My season of glory manifest, in Jesus name.

8. Blood of Jesus, convert my ridicule to miracle, in Jesus name.

9. Evil rope tying me down on evil altar, receive fire, in Jesus name.

10. My life, my glory, come out of the cage, in Jesus name.

11. Every evil word spoken against my glory that is affecting me now, be nullified in the name of Jesus.

12. I remove my name from the register of born-for-nothing, in Jesus name.

13. Cycle of poverty in my family line, break, in Jesus name.

14. Every sickness programmed unto death and fashioned against my life, I shake you out of my life, in Jesus name.

15. My life, hear the word of your maker, move forward, in Jesus name.

16. Blood of Jesus, set me free from the cage of ancestral altars, in Jesus name.

17. Any glory terminator, destiny destroyer, assigned against me, die, in Jesus name.

Prayers to Experience 24 Hour Miracles

1. Favour that swallow shame, fall upon me, in the name of Jesus.

2. From today, poverty become history in my life, in Jesus name.

3. Oh Lord, by your consuming fire, destroy any evil plantation of darkness in my life, in Jesus name.

4. Every good thing the enemy stole from my life, I recover 7 folds by fire, in Jesus name.

5. Stranger of darkness hiding in my body, release me by fire by force, in Jesus name.

6. My divine timing for celebration, appear! in Jesus name.

7. Association of mockers gathered against me, scatter, in the name of Jesus.

8. Evil power contending against my moving forward, die, in Jesus name.

9. I withdraw my progress from evil altars, in Jesus name.

What is Your Destiny?

It is what God has assigned you to do in this world. Also it is your road map on this earth and what God has written concerning you. The greatest disaster is for a person to die and when he gets to heaven, he is told that he has not fulfilled his destiny.

Don't wait until you are told you have 3 days to live on earth before you take action. The enemy fights tooth and nail to make sure that you are frustrated. Say these Prayer Points with holy anger:

1. Any power, assigned to waste my life, wherever you are, die!!!

2. The plan of the wicked over my destiny, scatter.

3. Any troubler of my destiny, your time is up, die.

4. In Jesus name, I shall fulfil my destiny. Whether your enemy likes it or not, you will fulfill your destiny.

5. Any power commissioned to kill me, die in my place, in Jesus name.

6. Any wicked evil prison where the enemy has kept me, I come out by fire.

The Lord will add beauty and colour to your destiny in Jesus name. You shall see, enjoy and sit on your throne of celebration, whether the enemy likes it or not. Rivers flow and make a way for itself whenever there is an obstacle before it. These two rivers we shall discuss are opposite each other. Life is divided also into two and is a choice for you to make. A person can choose either the negative or the positive side of life.

Deuteronomy 30:19 *"I call heaven and earth to record this day against you, that I have set before you life and death, blessing and cursing: therefore choose life, that both thou and thy seed may live"*

The two rivers run concurrently. These rivers are River Blessings and River Curses. You can choose one only.

Deuteronomy 27:12 *"These shall stand upon mount Ger'-i-zim to bless the people, when ye are come over Judah; and Is'-sachar, and Joseph, and Benjamin"*

The job of a priest is to pronounce blessings or curses. The first mountain talked about in the verse is Mt. Gerizen (a mountain of blessing). The second mountain is Mt. Ebar (a mountain of curses). They are side by side. There are some people who want to remain surface Christians (lukewarm). Don't, "for he will spew you out of his mouth Rev. 3:16. The worst place to stay is in the middle of the road, for it is very dangerous.

Deuteronomy 7:13-14 *"And he will love thee, and bless thee, and multiply thee: he will also bless the fruit of thy womb, and the fruit of thy land, thy corn, and thy wine, and thine oil, the increase of thy kine, and the flocks of thy sheep, in the land which he sware unto thy fathers to give thee. Thou shalt be blessed above all people: there shall not be male or female barren among you, or among your cattle."*

Deuteronomy 28:1 *"And it shall come to pass, if thou shalt hearken diligently unto the voice of the LORD thy GOD, to observe and to do all his commandments which I command thee this day, that the LORD will set thee on high above all nations of the earth."*

Blessing is good and that was the first contact that man had with God. There are invisible laws that govern this world. There are people who don't come to the Lord, still they prosper. There are things you need to do to be blessed. You have to follow the principles. Don't do evil but do well, for whatever a man sows, that he shall reap. God is a non-partial God and rewards good for good.

The second river is the river of curses

Nobody wants to be cursed. Curses bring afflictions,

calamities, pains, despair, tormentors of destiny and can kill.

A curse is a strong word angrily expressed against a person. This is the cause of spiritual limitation. It can limit and imprison a person. That is why many suffer and are under affliction.

Proverbs 26:2 *"As the bird by wandering, as the swallow by flying, so the curse causeless shall not come"*

This means that a curse does not come if you don't merit it. If you don't break the hedge serpent will not bite. If you live a holy life no curse placed by anyone can stand. But if you break the hedge, you will be bitten by a serpent. We shall see why the enemy gets us.

THE CAUSES OF CURSES

What causes a curse to come about?

1. **Sins of the Previous Generations:** Ex. 20:5. "Thou shall not bow down thyself to them, nor serve them: for I the LORD thy God, am a jealous God, visiting the iniquity of the fathers upon the children unto the third and fourth generation of them that hate me;..."

We are not expected to serve idols of any sort, for it is an embarrassment to God. But this was the first sin of our fathers. Every African has a great work to do under this effect. For our fathers devised and practiced wicked juju powers. They worshipped idols and the effects are what we are seeing today.

Proverbs 3:13 *"Happy is the man that findeth wisdom and the man that getteth understanding"*

God does not play with this. The worst is that some

educated and some Christians still relate with these. A land that worships idols can never move forward. Identify any form of identification with idol worship in your life and remove it. Some wear a cross signifying where Jesus is still hanging on. Some in the name of decoration buy idols into their houses.

Acts 19:18-19 *"And many that believed came and confessed and showed their deeds"*

Reject and remove all these idols. Some Christians still enjoy seeing pictures, which they took when they were unbelievers.

2. **Curses of the elders:**

Elders are to be highly respected but our modern world don't recognize this. The scripture says, *"Rebuke not an elder but entreat him as a father and the younger men as brethren".* (1 Timothy 5:1)

Many of us rebuke our elders and disrespect them. Some have suffered tragedy and backwardness because they broke God's law.

Lamentations 4:16 *"The anger of the LORD hath divided them; he will no more regard them: they respected not the persons of the priests, they favoured not the elders"*

We have allowed modernity and education to take the blessings attached to this away from us. We also need to respect men of God. The children who disrespected Elisha were devoured by hungry lions through the curse from the man of God.

3. **Curse of Non-tithers:**

You must give God His own share or you will suffer for it. A brother continued eating his tithe until his mouth started swelling up. He ran back to the church and paid his tithe, suddenly, the swollen mouth vanished. To some, it may be business setback, wayward children, or sickness, God must take his tithe from you. If you don't pay your tithe directly, you will be paying it indirectly. May the Lord deliver us.

4. **Neglect of the Poor:**

A country that takes care of the poor are termed developed. It is your responsibility to take care of the poor, widows, orphans and the helpless.

5. **Professional Misconduct:**

Consider the following examples:

a) The Doctors, who are greedy. They choose to refer safe delivery to delivery through operation because it will bring more money. One sister had a very serious sickness and went to a doctor. In her affliction, the doctor almost raped her in place of offering medication.

b) The Police, they arrest the innocent and run away from the guilty.

c) The Politicians, they share the money that would have

been used to fulfill their promises. They construct fake roads.

d) The Pastors, some wolfs and the sheep have allowed corruption into the church and joined hands to make people suffer, just for the love of money.

e) The handi-workers / craftsmen, they forge and lie to make money. Some teachers go to school 2 days in a week while they are paid for a full week. The marketers always heighten the price of goods to make gains and still lie about the cost price. They put the rotten ones under and the good ones on top. Some tailors also demand for four (4) yards of cloth from their customers for a cloth in which 3 yards can sew, with the intention to use 1 yard to sew for their children. Some labourers, are not duly paid by wicked masters and these masters bring curses in turn by either the labourers or their victims' families and well wish-ers. Some Business Partners rob themselves. One of them may decide to rob the other to be on the top, forgetting the prior agreement.

All these acts can cause causes to be released against a person.

8

WAY OF ESCAPE FROM CURSES

How can one escape curses?

1. Forgiveness:

When the issues of curses are mentioned, Forgiveness is important. Ask for forgiveness if you have cheated. Turn away from it and refuse to cheat again.

2. Restitution:

Decide never to do evil again so that a curse will not have a cause. For a causeless curse shall not stand. Repent from evil or sin and receive Jesus into your life today, then, you can break those curses. If you can be sincere and open up to God today, He will accept you. Flee from evil.

Prayer Points

1. Lord, am sorry for my sins, forgive me.

2. Blood of Jesus, wash me and heal me.

3. Let my destiny and family be healed in Jesus name.

4. Every generational curse in charge of my problem, Break.

5. Yoke-breaking power of God, fall upon me.

6. Satan and his evil prophecy over my life, die!

7. Jesus, Jesus, Jesus appear in my battle field today, Amen.

8. My season of double celebration appear, in the name of Jesus

9. Every angry altar fashioned against my life, receive Holy Ghost fire.

10. My breakthrough, hear the word of the Lord, jump out of evil altar, in Jesus name.

Specific Prayers to Break Curses

1. Blood of Jesus, I renounce every generational curse placed upon my life, in Jesus name.

2. Every curse of sudden death over my life, break!

3. Every curse of working for others to eat, break, in Jesus name.

4. Evil marriage curses in my life, break in Jesus name.

5. Blood of Jesus, redeem my past and bless my future.

6. The foundation of evil stronghold of curses, I pull you down.

7. Curses that waste destiny, my life is not for you, release me, break in Jesus name.

8. Every curse of tragedy and calamity, break in Jesus name.

9. Oh God, arise and waste my waster

10. Evil king, sitting on the throne of my life, I dethrone you, in Jesus name.

11. Every curse of seeing good thing and not enjoying it, break, in Jesus name.

12. The wickedness of the wicked in my life, expire.

13. Owner of curses, sicknesses, afflictions, carry your loads, in Jesus name.

14. Every wealth and riches stolen from me, I recover now, in Jesus name.

9

DELIVERANCE FROM EVIL, SPIRITUAL BUS STOP

Read the following scriptures:

Psalm 2:1-12

Psalm 7:6

There are people whose disturbers can only be disturbed by God. The Lord can defend his Children. Today, the Lord will arise and defend his interest in your life and break the teeth of your destroyers. Point your right hand to the heaven and say these prayers:

1. O God! arise in your anger and fight for me today, in Jesus name.

2. Any raging battle against my life, die!

3. Every angry altar delegated against my life, catch fire.

I decree that any altar that has collected evil sacrifices against you will catch fire and release all their captives.

Whenever you feel pains, it is a sign that the system is not in order and it calls for attention. There are people who are no longer moving forward because they have stopped in an evil bus-stop. If you are no longer enjoying life the way you ought to, you have to move away from that evil bus-stop.

Exodus 33:1 *"And the LORD said unto Moses, Depart and go up hence, thou and the people which thou hast brought up out of the land of Egypt, unto the land which I sware unto Abraham, to Isaac, and to Jacob, saying, Unto thy seed will I give it"*

To you who are not in your right bus-stop, I command you to depart and go up. Some people may depart and go to the wrong place. Say this: *"My destiny, life and business, depart from evil bus-stop and go to where there is no distur- bances and confusion"*.

Upstairs is filled with pleasure. Any power that wants to keep you where your destiny will suffer shall die!

10

INSIGHTS INTO EVIL BUS STOPS

There is nothing wrong being at a bus-stop, for it is a connection to the next level. Bus-stop is not a place of habitation but a place of loading and offloading, where the new is connected with the old. Life is not meant to be stagnant so you are meant to move forward.

Deuteronomy 1:6 *"The LORD our GOD spake unto us in Ho'reb, saying, Ye have dwelt long enough in this mount"*

God is a God of movement and progress. Everything in the world continues to develop, for change is constant in life. Some people are like hard concrete, they are static. Remember that still water is deadly. You must move forward, for God is always ready to do a new thing. You must decide to be moving forward spiritually and physically. You must not be stagnant. Life is very short. Some people refuse change because of the fear of the unknown, yet changes always bring progress. Frustration is a sign of something wrong. Avoid it.

A father followed his son to an end of year send-forth. As prizes were being given to brilliant pupils with applauses, his father said to him, 'these are real sons." At the end of the ceremony, while they were waiting for a means to go at a bus-stop, seeing other parents carrying their children in their cars drive past them, the boy equally said to him, "Daddy, these are real parents."

If you want your children to progress, you also should desire progress. If you don't want your children to be sluggish, don't be one either.

1 Chronicles 4:9 *"And Jabez was more honourable than his brethren: and his mother called his name Jabez, saying, because I bare him with sorrow"*

Jabez was more honourable than his brethren but still, his life was a mess. He stood up and spoke to the Lord, saying that his case must change. Some people answer good names but. the reverse is the case in their lives, those names being used to mock them.

Say this: *"I reject every evil identity. There are certain situations you must not accept."*

11

HOW TO IDENTIFY EVIL BUS STOPS

Here are 2 ways of identifying evil bus stops:

1. A Life of Dependence

Acts 3:2 *"And a certain man lame from his mother's womb was carried, whom they laid daily at the gate of the temple which is called Beautiful to ask alms of them that entered into the temple"*

Are you still squatting and patching things up when you are expected to be mature and successful, then you have to reject it. Some people are born into negatively sided family and this has been the cause of their problem.

Mark 10:46 *"And they came to Jericho: and as he went out of Jericho with his disciples and a great number of people, blind Bartmaeus, the son of Timaeus, sat by the highway side begging."*

This is another evil bus-stop. Some people have been

known and marked beggars even in the church. What an evil bus-stop! Luckily, you will receive deliverance from this bus- stop. Anybody under or on evil bus-stop lives a life of dependence.

2. A lot of Suffering

Mark 5:25 *"And a certain woman, which had an issue of blood twelve years,..."*

They encounter constant suffering and affliction.

Say: "I reject every evil identity, in Jesus name."

Psalm 137:1 *"By the rivers of Babylon, there we sat down, yea, we wept when we remembered Zion." They were in an evil bus- stop.*

One day, Jacob recognized that his condition does not rhyme with his name, so he sought God's face.

Say this: "Father! align my name with the content of my destiny"

Most people have good names but the reverse is often the case in their lives. To be in the cage of an enemy is tantamount to being in an evil bus- stop which is evidenced by backwardness in life.

12

CONDITIONS THAT PROMPT EVIL BUS STOPS

Here are some of the conditions that prompt evil bus stops:

1. Cobweb

Spiritual things are very interesting and dynamic. Some people are very articulate but when they are to be applauded, they would be condemned. Some toil day and night in vain. Cobweb is a sign of coverage. This cobweb covers one's beauty, good works and hard work but today, any cobweb against you shall be roasted by fire.

2. Evil Rope

Mark 11:2 *"And said unto them, go your way into the village over against you: and as soon as ye be entered into it, ye shall find a colt tied, whereon never man sat; loose him and bring him"*

There are people whom Jesus shall send to lose you and

you shall be set free. The horse has been tied there for long and this notwithstanding, when Jesus came to lose it, people still asked silly questions, intending that the horse should remain there. Any evil rope tying you to that evil bus-stop shall catch fire.

3. Sin

Per Judges 16:4, we can see that the enemy dealt so badly with Samson because he came into an evil bus-stop (Delilah = Sin). Sin in the life of Samson took him to the evil bus-stop where he was killed. A strong man of war turned into a strong man that grinds and a thing of scorn.

Certainly, one thing that destroys people's destinies quickly is the sin of fornication and adultery.

13

ESCAPE FROM EVIL BUS STOPS

If you want to escape from evil bus stops, there are actions that you need to take and there are specific prayers you need to pray.

Actions Required for Escaping Evil Bus Stops

(1) Repent and give your life to Jesus Christ.

(2) Depart from Sin (Psalm 66:18)

(3) Cry out to be heard like blind Bartimeus, Samson and Jabez. God does not reject a holy cry. For a broken and apologetic heart, the Lord does not despise.

Specific Prayers Against Evil Bus Stops

1. Father, align my name with your predestined destiny for my life.

2. Anything in my life that does not glorify God (sickness,

barrenness, poverty, suffering, rejection, homelessness, failure, late marriage) DIE!!!.

3. Lord Jesus, by your consuming fire, destroy oppression in my life.

4. Anything that oppose blessing in my life, wither away.

5. Untimely death is not my portion, in Jesus name.

6. Oh God, arise and bless me after the order of Abraham, Isaac and Jacob.

7. The pregnancy of the wicked over my life, be aborted in Jesus name.

8. Evil rope tying me down, break

9. Satan, take your hands off my destiny now, in Jesus name.

10. Satan give me back what you have stolen from me.

11. Enemy of progress, release me now in Jesus name.

12. Oh Lord, bring me face to face with true helpers.

13. Every money consuming sickness, dry up by fire, in Jesus name.

14. Road blocking power, clear yourself out of my way.

15. Any power introducing delay in my journey in life, Fall down and die.

16. Evil powers blocking answers to my prayers, be wasted today.

17. Any power making it difficult for me to move forward, die.

18. Lord Jesus, break my yoke.

Specific Prayers of Deliverance from Stagnancy

1. Cobweb of limitation, release me by fire.

2. Evil voice binding me, wither in Jesus name.

3. Evil chain tying me down at evil bus stop, break by fire.

4. Every coven decision made against my progress, scatter in Jesus name.

5. Evil altar, caging my life, glory and destiny, release me by fire.

6. Every instrument of bewitchment working against my life, scatter.

7. Network of witchcraft in my family house, be exposed, be disgraced.

8. Evil power behind my continuous suffering, die!

9. Embargo power, release me, in Jesus name.

10. Evil hand chasing good things away from me, wither.

11. Any power that has vowed that I will not see good things, you are a liar, die!

12. Prosperity blocker, fashioned against me, die!

14

RECEIVING THE POWER TO OBTAIN AND RETAIN

Before we look at the meat of this chapter, say the following prayer points loud and clear:

1. Anything representing me in any evil altar, receive Fire.

2. Holy Ghost, empower me to stand in life, in Jesus name. The stronghold of the enemy shall be pulled down in Jesus name.

Now, to obtain and retain is the major problem in the life of people. Some can't retain the blessings of God either by the influence of a power or their carelessness. You shall be retaining your blessings from today in Jesus name.

Ephesians 1:3 *"Blessed be the God and Father of our Lord Jesus Christ, Who hath blessed us with all spiritual blessings in heavenly places in Christ. Every time we gather in the presence of God, He loads us with benefits and blessings. God has been blessing us but the question is, 'where are those blessings'?"*

2 Peter 1:3 *"According as his divine power hath given unto us all things that pertain unto life and godliness, through the knowledge of him that called us to glory and virtue."*

These things that God gives us are the things that help us enjoy this world. (Cars, houses, good health). There are some people who have actually come in contact with great riches but where are those riches? They were not retained. We serve God because He is a Father who blesses His children that walk in obedience.

Where are those blessings that God has been promising? Does it mean that He is no more fulfilling those promises again? He fulfils His promises but our enemies steal them out from us. God blesses us so that we can retain those blessings and not to lose them.

Judges 2:6 *"And when Joshua had let the people go, the children of Israel went every man unto his inheritance to possess the land."*

God's blessings are meant to be permanent. God wants you to possess what belongs to you but the problem is that some can't retain those blessings. There are some that spiritually have holes and basket pockets. All their struggling and hustling are being wasted but God will block all holes that devour your labour. The rate at which people loose is greater than the rate they possess but God will give you power that will enable you to obtain and retain all in Jesus name. Shout: I receive power to obtain and retain (7 times).

Wealth and opportunities come across some people's ways but they weren't able to retain them. There are some that don't know how to keep their marriages. When Jesus met the Samaritan woman, the woman was made to thirst for the living water because she truly can't keep her marriage and had dated 6 men.

There are some that spiritual and wicked powers manipulate their successes so that they can't retain their God's given position. There are some who married but now, they are single because the spirit of tragedy and frustration is working against their lives. For some people, when money comes their way or enters into their hands, unknown and unplanned situations would come up to devour the money and disappears when the money has finished.

A question was thrown to Jesus about a woman who had married 7 brothers, each of them dying mysteriously. What happened to the woman to the extent of losing 7 marriages? The spirit of tragedy!

Any power that is closing the factory of your success, that wants you to labour in vain, shall be swallowed up by the ground and destroyed, in Jesus name.

God does not want you to loose that which you have obtained from Him but to retain it. There are some people whose blessings are terminated right from the dream. These are anti-harvest forces. There are so many people who continue to labour in building a house but die immediately the house is completed. Some people dream about where they are squandering money immediately they are about to get good money. This means that spiritually, the money that they are about to possess has already been spent, therefore even when they get the money physically, it would be of no benefit. Whatever power that is behind get and loose in your life is destroyed, in Jesus name.

Why Get and Lose?

What makes a person get and then lose?

1. Activities of Evil Altars: When there is a cry against you from an evil altar, the spirit of get and loose comes to stop your retentive ability and make your blessings slippery. Today! They shall be destroyed!

2. Failure in Tithes and Offerings: If you steal from God, He will, send devourers to torment you. Some of you make promises and pledges to God, vow even but don't pay up.

Then came the word of the LORD by Haggai the prophet saying, Is it time for you O ye, to dwell in your ceiled houses, and this house lie waste? Ye have sown much, and bring in little; ye eat, but ye have not enough; ye drink, but ye are not filled with drink; ye clothe you but there is none warm; and he that earneth wages earneth wages to put it into a bag with holes Haggai 1:3,4,6.

3. Examine your ways: Those who don't pay their tithes are never balanced. Pay your tithe, pay your offerings.

4. Evil names that people bear: There are some people that bear names that can't bless them, names that don't please God. How can God find it easy to write down "Ekemezie"

(Eke market day did me good) into the book of life. It means that it wasn't God that brought you into this world. What a malicious name!

5. Sin: This is an aborter of glory. Sin is a hedge breaker for the enemy and he must come in and bite.

6. Lack of effective prayer to sustain your blessings: Some stop praying whenever a certain blessing comes into their hands. It takes prayers to sustain good things in your hands.

A prayer warrior got a white collar job of great level and stopped praying until one day, he got to the office, where he has been working hard and does not pervert justice;. He was called and sacked just because he had enemies who don't appreciate his sincerity and truth. He rushed back to the church and the pastor gave him prayer points which he prayed seriously.

When he got to the office the second day, he was apologized to by his boss and was promoted to another level. Some people stop attending church activities whenever they are blessed and rush back to God when the enemy starts fighting. Who are we doing, God or ourselves?

If you don't have Jesus, you can't get and keep your blessings and then enemy would continue to be stealing from you. Give your life to Jesus Christ today and He will give you the power to obtain and retain.

———

Prayer Points

1. Activities of devourers in my finances, wither, in Jesus name,

2. All closed doors against me, open now in Jesus name.

3. Rock of Ages, fight for me today/

4. Arrow of internal suffering, release me in Jesus name.

5. part of my body that is under the control of evil power, be set free now in Jesus name.

6. Every evil plant that my God has not planted, be uprooted, in Jesus name.

7. I shall not die but live in Jesus name.

Specific Prayers to Obtain and Retain blessings

1. Every licking pocket, I seal you up by the blood of Jesus.

2. Activities of devourers in my life, Come to an end today.

3. Glory of God, my life is available, enter!

4. Marine spirit, stealing from me, wither.

5. Evil marks in my body, I rub you off by the blood of Jesus.

6. Whether my enemy likes it or not, I will celebrate.

7. I shall not labour for another to eat, in Jesus name.

8. I shall not build for others to inhabit

9. Spirit of emptier in my life, pack your loads and go.

10. Any power blocking good things from coming to me, die!

11. All my hanging blessings, I receive you now in Jesus name.

12. Evil gang up against my glory, scatter to desolation.

13. Wherever I have failed before now, I will succeed in Jesus name.

14. My life, hear the word of the Lord, reject evil arrow, in Jesus name.

15. Blood of Jesus, sanitize my life.

16. The rage of unrepentant wickedness against me, expire!

Here are some of the other books written by Ladejola Abiodun:

The God of Possibility

You Cannot Give Up Now

No More Delay

Made in United States
Troutdale, OR
10/22/2023

13928306R00037